MINDFULNESS
IN 8 DAYS

HOW TO FIND INNER PEACE IN A WORLD OF STRESS AND ANXIETY

KATHIRASAN K

Marshall Cavendish
Editions

© 2017 K. Kathirasan and Marshall Cavendish International (Asia) Pte Ltd

Published in 2017 by Marshall Cavendish Editions
An imprint of Marshall Cavendish International
1 New Industrial Road, Singapore 536196

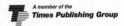

A member of the
Times Publishing Group

Other Marshall Cavendish Offices:
Marshall Cavendish Corporation. 99 White Plains Road, Tarrytown NY 10591–9001, USA • Marshall Cavendish International (Thailand) Co Ltd. 253 Asoke, 12th Flr, Sukhumvit 21 Road, Klongtoey Nua, Wattana, Bangkok 10110, Thailand • Marshall Cavendish (Malaysia) Sdn Bhd, Times Subang, Lot 46, Subang Hi-Tech Industrial Park, Batu Tiga, 40000 Shah Alam, Selangor Darul Ehsan, Malaysia.

Marshall Cavendish is a registered trademark of Times Publishing Limited

National Library Board, Singapore Cataloguing-in-Publication Data
Name(s): Kathirasan, K.
Title: Mindfulness in 8 Days : How to find inner peace in a world of
        stress and anxiety / Kathirasan K.
Description: Singapore : Marshall Cavendish Editions, 2017.
Identifier(s): OCN 966653728 | ISBN 978-981-4771-91-7 (paperback)
Subject(s): LCSH: Mindfulness (Psychology) | Stress management. |
        Meditation. | Well-being.
Classification: DDC 158.12--dc23

Printed in Singapore by Fabulous Printers Pte Ltd

CONTENTS

FOREWORD

Mindfulness is about cultivating awareness of the present moment, so that we can meet ourselves and others with kindness and compassion.

Compassion is the key to a happier, more meaningful and peaceful life. Without being present, you can't hope to cultivate this quality.

In this book, Kathirasan guides you on a journey of mindfulness and compassion over eight transformative days. Eight days may seem like a short time, but ultimately you don't even need eight days. You just need this moment.

Right now, and in every waking moment, you have the choice to be consciously aware of the outer world and your inner land-scape, or to go back to thinking down those well-worn neural highways of your mind. Thoughts about what you have to do, or what you should have done. How good you are or how bad you are. And all the time, in front of your very eyes, a unique miracle is unfolding.

With well-chosen quotes, wise words of encouragement, and easy-to-do daily activities, this book will awaken your senses, calm your mind and open your heart to a more nourishing and sustainable way of living.

You're in for a treat!

Shamash Alidina
Author of *The Mindful Way Through Stress*
and *Mindfulness for Dummies*

INTRODUCTION

This book is probably one of the shortest manuals you will find on understanding and practising mindfulness.

Mindfulness is the art of living in the present moment without losing focus on the future. It allows us to be self-aware while we go about the affairs of our lives.

The rewards of mindfulness practices are twofold:

1. Research has shown that mindfulness can greatly reduce stress levels and help regulate negative emotions.

2. By cultivating self-awareness, mindfulness practices can enhance our performance, both personal and professional.

I was first introduced to mindfulness and meditation in the late 1990s by a Himalayan teacher. It had a tremendous impact on me, transforming my worldview and my perceptions of success and failure, stress and joy.

I was at that time a very unhappy person. In trying to cope with life's challenges, I had ended up in a state of constantly wanting *more* in terms of everything I experienced.

I wanted people to love me, I wanted success and to be recognised for it, I wanted to be rich.

Pursuing these goals left me stressed and eventually depressed. I was demanding so much from myself and demanding so much from the world.

And all that time, I did not know who, or what, I was. Everything I knew of myself was defined through the eyes of others.

After learning mindfulness, all this changed. I became more self-aware, and with that came the ability to confront difficult situations with poise, and to treat myself and others with more compassion.

Where I once demanded so much of the world, I now discovered joy within. In fact, I started discovering aspects of myself which I never knew existed.

These changes positively influenced my career, my emotional health, and the relationships I had with other people.

I gained a new clarity of purpose and an understanding of the different roles I played in life. With mindfulness, I also found a renewed appreciation for everything the world had to offer.

These changes led me to start teaching mindfulness practices, long before they entered mainstream media.

Most of the people who came to my courses looked weary, dissatisfied, conflicted, or lost. By the time they were midway through the programme, almost everyone said that their life had taken a noticeable positive turn.

Some started appreciating their spouse more. Some started to notice behaviours that were contrary to values they held close to their hearts. More than a few told me that they finally knew who they were.

And all that I taught them was not to change, but to just *notice the change*. By merely noticing and observing, change happened for them.

Hence, I decided to write this book as an offering to the world, to encourage you to experience mindfulness in your everyday life.

I have met people who are skeptical about mindfulness, assuming it to be another New Age fad. I resonate strongly with them, as it is better to approach any practice with skepticism until it is proven to be valuable to you.

Mindfulness has been one of the most researched contemplative sciences of the last two decades. With increasing evidence of its effectiveness, you may be more inclined to try out some mindfulness practices.

Or perhaps you wish to know what mindfulness is before embarking on a full-fledged intensive programme.

I have written this book for those of you who seek:

- a glimpse into the world of mindfulness before taking the journey

- a structured and self-paced mindfulness experience

- a private journey in mindfulness

This book takes the form of eight experiments with yourself over eight days.

Just as there is no one solution that can solve all of the world's problems, there is no one path for everyone to take. You have to find your own path. This book will help you along the way.

Here is an opportunity for you to enter into the world of mindfulness in the privacy of your own home, your office or even on your daily commute.

You can take things at your own pace – you don't have to do all eight days in a row.

The only thing I ask is that you approach these practices with an attitude of open-mindedness and a willingness to experiment. Be like a toddler that ventures to experience everything in its path with genuine curiosity.

I wish you wellness and joy on this journey.

DAY 1

THE AUTOPILOT

You are on a flight to your holiday destination. The pilot has welcomed everyone onboard, introduced his co-pilot and crew, and announced the estimated arrival time.

You sit back and relax.

Little do you realise, apart from the pilot and co-pilot, there is another pilot in the cockpit with them – a non-human one, the 'autopilot'.

This pilot has no heart, and neither does he have a brain like yours.

'HE WHO KNOWS OTHERS IS WISE;
HE WHO KNOWS HIMSELF
IS ENLIGHTENED'

– LAO TZU

And yet he knows your destination like the back of his hand and needs no control from the human pilots.

The moment the pilots get into the cockpit, the autopilot is just a switch away. All the pilots need to do is to switch him on, and the autopilot works his magic.

We, too, have an autopilot in the pit of our brain.

Our autopilot manifests when we do things in a mechanical manner without mindful awareness.

Do you brush your teeth feeling the bristles of the toothbrush on your gums and teeth?

Do you shower feeling the contact of water on your skin and feeling the touch of your hands as you soap yourself?

Or do you cruise through these daily activities with your mind on other thoughts?

Your autopilot, although it steers you through these activities safely, prevents you from being fully in the moment.

You could be reading the newspapers and upon finishing you realise you finished a whole cup of tea without any recollection of tasting it at all.

When you are on autopilot, you deprive yourself of the opportunity to fully experience and enjoy the journey called life.

Worse still, without being aware of it, your thoughts and actions may be hijacked by this autopilot.

Recall a situation when someone said 'no' to an idea or suggestion of yours. Your mind may have assumed that the 'no' was a sign of rejection in spite of knowing it was actually just a simple 'no' to your idea and not you as a person.

This is again your autopilot in action. It can prevent you from seeing what is there and replace it with what is not there.

The autopilot has taken over our lives, and we cannot seem to take back possession.

Now, I must qualify that the autopilot is not a bad guy all the time. In times of emergency and danger, he does help by making quick decisions to save us.

But when we have our autopilot in the 'on' position all the time, we lose our attentiveness to our daily affairs, such that we do not remember the journey anymore. All we are interested in is the destination.

One of the key purposes of mindfulness is to allow you to reclaim the driver's seat and start being fully there in every moment and every experience.

The simplest way to do this is not to fight your autopilot but to gently start with practices that focus your attention on the present moment.

You can pay attention to almost anything in your life. All you need is an intentional mind wanting to pay attention to any experience or activity.

The simplest of things can be magnified into something profound just by paying attention to them. Imagine the experience

'MINDFULNESS MEANS PAYING ATTENTION IN A PARTICULAR WAY; ON PURPOSE, IN THE PRESENT MOMENT, AND NON-JUDGMENTALLY.'

– JON KABAT-ZINN

of scientists when they first looked into the microscope to study the pollen in plants.

By paying attention to your own body, thoughts and emotions, you come to a better understanding of yourself and your relationships with other people in your life.

Mindfulness helps us to recognise the value of the present moment, which we often miss while going about 'living' our lives.

But are we really 'living' our lives at all?

So busy are we moving from one task to another, we forget to value each moment. I could be so wrapped up in answering an office email at home that I ignored my child right next to me yearning for my attention.

We are more often mere passersby of our own lives rather than people who are truly living.

On my own mindfulness journey, I have stopped looking for a purpose for living my life.

Instead, I find that the purpose is 'in the living' rather than in 'seeking' an answer. When I dropped that search, I suddenly started living my life more purposefully and meaningfully.

Mindfulness is the beginning of living and the end to searching.

How is it that such a simple thing as paying attention has become so difficult?

Have you seen how infants crawl and pick up objects to observe as if they have never seen these objects before?

In fact, that's exactly what it is, they have never seen those things before. That innocent, childlike curiosity is what we have lost.

The child cries only when it is hungry; it doesn't cry because of, say, a lack of food in storage for tomorrow. The child is only

'YESTERDAY'S THE PAST,
TOMORROW'S THE FUTURE, BUT
TODAY IS A GIFT. THAT'S WHY
IT'S CALLED THE PRESENT.'

– BIL KEANE

interested in the present, exploring and experiencing whatever life presents.

Imagine how it would be if this childlike curiosity that is grounded in the present moment could be coupled with the maturity of our adult life experiences. This is definitely a recipe for a great mindful life.

And yet, we often neglect the present moment, obsessed as we are with the future and the past.

We fail to realise that the present moment is what creates the past in the form of memories. The same present moment forms the reference plane for our thinking about the future.

The present moment is free from both anxiety and regrets, as all the regrets and sorrows we carry are centred in the past, while all our anxieties and worries are centred in the future.

The present moment is also without time because you cannot measure it. Try picking up a stopwatch and measuring how long it takes to be 'present'. The moment the clock starts ticking it has become the past.

You cannot hold on to the present moment either.

All that we can do is just *be* in the present moment.

HOW TO BE MINDFUL

The first step towards being mindful is to bring three principles into your life:

1. Have the **intention** to be mindful

2. Pay **attention** to things and experiences

3. Cultivate a healthy **attitude** towards life experiences

These are the three core principles of mindfulness. They are the *foundations* for consistent and rewarding practice, as well as the *fruits* of practice.

Mindfulness is an ongoing process, not a finite goal. So don't approach mindfulness as another item in your checklist to be accomplished. Rather, make it a way of living.

See mindfulness like the way you breathe.

Do you have to make a petition every day for your lungs to breathe for your well-being or does it just happen?

Do you have to consciously make your breathing heavy when you go for a run or does it happen naturally?

Many things in nature just happen, like the sun rising and setting. Natural phenomena do not have an agenda like us humans. They are not motivated by rewards and successes.

Mindfulness is best appreciated when you have no real agenda other than being mindful. It is indeed a way of living and being yourself, with yourself.

1. THE INTENTION TO BE MINDFUL

Finding your intention behind the desire to learn and practise mindfulness is an important discovery. Ask yourself the following questions:

1. What do I understand by mindfulness?

2. Why do I want to be mindful?

3. What benefits do I hope to get by practising mindfulness?

Your answers will provide direction on your mindfulness journey, like a compass. They will provide greater clarity about your values, vision and goals in life.

There are no wrong answers to these questions as there could be many reasons for a single action. My intention for mindfulness could be anything from wanting to be healthy to perhaps just wanting to be myself.

While we set our intentions, we do need to expect that they may change from time to time. That is perfectly normal.

2. PAYING ATTENTION

Paying attention is the pivot on which all mindfulness practices rest. It involves concentrating the mind on a particular object or experience over a length of time.

Remember that we can choose what to pay attention to.

For example, if you had to take a train journey to visit your disagreeable mother-in-law, it would be normal for you to dread the train ride.

But the truth of the matter is that your mother-in-law is not on the train with you. She is part of the future, not part of the present moment.

So 'be' on the train ride and not drifting to the visit ahead. Pay attention to the green fields, the activity within the train cabin, your own breathing. This is an opportunity for being with yourself instead of transporting yourself to the future or a place where you are yet to be.

This book will show you how to practise the skill of paying attention in particular ways.

3. A HEALTHY ATTITUDE

Your mindfulness journey will be a much smoother and more rewarding one if you have the right attitude. The right attitude will also keep you on a steady path on your journey in the long run.

It has been said that 'Your attitude determines your altitude' – attitude can make a whole lot of difference. It is like that pinch of salt that makes a dish so tasty.

'YOUR LIVING IS DETERMINED NOT
SO MUCH BY WHAT LIFE BRINGS TO YOU
AS BY THE ATTITUDE YOU BRING TO
LIFE; NOT SO MUCH BY WHAT HAPPENS
TO YOU AS BY THE WAY YOUR MIND
LOOKS AT WHAT HAPPENS.'

– KHALIL GIBRAN

Here are some healthy attitudes that are worth cultivating:

Acceptance

Acceptance is the most helpful attitude for helping you secure the continuous practice of mindfulness. It is about accepting any experience that arises with accommodation and non-judgment.

It is certain that during your mindfulness practices your mind may wander or your body aches may prevent you from doing certain movements.

The attitude of acceptance will allow you to accept these short-comings, and march on with your practice.

Acceptance also relates to being in the present without comparing your practice with the past or with your ideals of the future.

This also means that you don't compare your practices with the practices of others. You are unique and so is your life a unique one. There is no better reason than this for you to not compare but to accept yourself as you are.

Learner's mind

Cultivating the attitude of a learner will allow you to see things anew in every practice. It also prevents you from comparing or benchmarking your current practice with the past.

Tell yourself that you are always learning every time you start your practice.

And tell yourself that you are always a work-in-progress. In fact, all of us are. This humility is born of the understanding that there is no 'real' goal to be achieved other than being what we are.

The learner in me will always allow me to be an adventurer instead of a gold miner.

Focusing on what works

We are frequently bent on seeking out things that do not work for us and fixing them. This fault-finding behaviour and the fear of failure can keep us from maturing emotionally.

In mindfulness we need to focus more on what is working for us in the practices than what is not.

All of us are individually unique and hence we need the ability to latch onto what works for us. There is no one-size-fits-all approach. As you practise, you will likely find that some of the practices resonate stronger with you than other practices.

Trust

In spite of all the empirical evidence that mindfulness works, you might doubt it in moments when your mind gets distracted, sleepy or bored.

In such moments, your trust in the process of mindfulness will keep you going.

Read up on the journeys of other mindfulness practitioners and their results – you can find numerous first-hand accounts in books and on the internet. Their stories will inspire you to trust this way of being.

Curiosity

Paying attention becomes a quest for knowledge when it is filled with curiosity.

This curiosity may lead you to discover new insights about your body, thoughts, behaviour, emotions and environment — all of which you might never have noticed before.

Curiosity is like a mirror that gets cleaned of its dust and tarnish with every practice, reflecting your being more and more accurately.

After every practice, you walk out a new person.

Letting go

Letting go is the opposite of being in control.

It has been said that the mountains are as though in meditation, and so are the waters and earth. They support whatever animate and inanimate things they bear not by controlling but by just 'being'.

Similarly, there is no effort required in the practice of mindfulness. What's needed is to let go of the idea that you are in control.

Our need for control stems from our innate need for security. We like to control people, systems and the environment around us to manipulate our thoughts to feel secure. It is only natural to feel this way.

However, we should try to keep that insecurity away from our mindfulness practices by letting go of what happens during our practices and focusing on acceptance.

Positivity

Positivity is the degree of wholesome emotions that we enjoy in our lives. These emotions can be joy, calmness, love, amusement, etc.

There is a general sense of cheerfulness among people who are positive.

One of the ways you can bring positivity in your life is by being cheerful during your practices. Sport a smile on your face before you start each practice.

Patience

The world around us keeps repeating that 'Time waits for no one' and the race against time never ends from the moment we are born.

Mindfulness is not something that you should race for or struggle for. Or it will end up being another rat race.

Mindfulness is your being, and it is always available to one who is available to it. Hence, the intention behind your mindfulness practice may be realised tomorrow, next month or even after a lifetime of practice.

The key to continuous practice is patience and acceptance.

Kindness

While kindness is always assumed to be of more value when it is shown to others, it is equally important that one shows kindness to oneself.

'I PREFER YOU TO MAKE
MISTAKES IN KINDNESS THAN
WORK MIRACLES IN UNKINDNESS.'

– MOTHER TERESA

More often than not, we bring appraisals of our behaviour, thoughts and feelings into our mindfulness practices.

There are no standards of right behaviour, right thoughts or right feelings in mindfulness practices. With kindness, we accept all our bodily sensations, thoughts and emotions.

I personally find that once we are kind to ourselves, we begin very naturally to be kind to others.

Thankfulness

Be thankful every day for being you and for having the opportunity to practise mindfulness.

Be thankful to people around you for enabling you to have your private time with yourself. Bring thankfulness to even the smallest of acts that people do for you.

For example, I am thankful to the stranger at the mall who took the effort to smile at me.

I am thankful to my wife for helping me choose an appropriate shirt for a business meeting.

I am thankful to the birds outside my window for making sweet music in the mornings.

The list goes on and on...

PRACTICE 1

NOTICING WITH CURIOSITY

This practice can be done anytime, anywhere.

1. Start noticing the environment you are in.

2. Bring curiosity into the exploration.

3. You may notice people or things or perhaps the palm of your hand.

4. See them as if you have never seen them before.

5. Start noticing the tiny details that you normally do not notice.

6. Do this practice for about three minutes.

Post-practice questions

- What were your thoughts during the practice?

- Was it easy to be curious?

- Did you make judgements about the people and things that you noticed?

DAY 2

I AM NOT A

HUMAN DOING

It is in our nature to give value to things that may not have intrinsic value.

This is how we start hobbies like collecting stamps, figurines, or cards. The stamps by themselves are just tiny slips of paper with designs printed on them, but through our likes and dislikes we create value in them. We value some more than others.

This is exactly the reason why we choose to give great respect and adulation to the CEO of a company but don't do the same for the office cleaner.

While the roles of the CEO and the cleaner may be different, the individuals taking on the roles are fundamentally the same. Both of them wake up in the morning and wish for a great day. Both of them desire happiness in their lives and form relationships just like everyone else.

But we have judged the CEO to be of greater value than the cleaner.

How can we see beyond people's roles and view them non-judgmentally?

'I SPEAK TO EVERYONE IN THE SAME WAY, WHETHER HE IS THE GARBAGE MAN OR THE PRESIDENT OF THE UNIVERSITY.'

– ALBERT EINSTEIN

NON-JUDGMENTAL VISION

In my years in the corporate world and community work, I have encountered people from all walks of life, from the president of the country to people who have not been as fortunate as the average man in terms of their quality of life.

I have worked with prison inmates, the elderly in assisted-living homes, the financially challenged and the emotionally weary.

In my heart of hearts, my perception of all of them has been as human beings pure and simple, with the sole difference being their current situation. Today someone might be a prisoner but tomorrow or in the future perhaps he could be a successful businessman.

People may change, but their innate being does not change.

When interacting with people doing their jobs, I tell myself that I am relating to their functional roles. At the same time, I take care to maintain the non-judgmental vision that fundamentally we are all the same.

YOU ARE NOT THE ROLE

A CEO gets home after a long day at work and tells his wife to bring him a drink.

The wife retorts, 'Am I your secretary?'

Frustrated, he walks into his teenage daughter's room to see if she has been studying for her exams which are around the corner.

He finds her on her smartphone, and scolds her for not focusing on her exam preparations.

The daughter gets angry that she is being bossed around like his staff, who are always at his beck and call.

This is a classic illustration of how we bring our roles into spaces where they are not needed. Roles are not absolute, and neither are they forever. We pick a role up, and we can also let them go, if we know how to do that.

The role of a parent is born along with the birth of a child. A name is given with one's birth. A designation is born along with a job and its description.

Some roles last longer and some shorter. But the fact remains that the roles do not outlive your nature as a human being. The roles depend on you for existence, but you can exist independent of the roles.

Build a list of the various roles that you play on a given day (e.g. parent, child, employer, employee, friend, spouse) and reflect on each of them in terms of three factors:

1. How important is that role to you?

2. How much time and energy do you invest in that role?

3. Are demanding too much of yourself in that role?

Each of our roles has its limits. By being mindful of their limits, we can effortlessly maximise the effectiveness of each of our roles.

For example, when I enter my office, I am a member of staff, and I nurture and play that role. When I step out of the office, I am no longer a member of staff.

When I reach home, I should be mindful of being a parent, spouse, son or daughter.

I do not bring my role as a CEO home. Or else there will come a time when someone at home gives me a rude awakening.

It is perfectly fine to be the boss at your workplace and be bossed around at home. We need to learn to let go of our roles in the appropriate situations.

The ability naturally develops as we regard our roles as something that we have picked up and are ready to let go of when the need arises.

My mother expresses this role of dissociation very well in her native tongue. When she is ill, she doesn't say 'I am unwell'; she says, 'The body is unwell'.

To me, this is a priceless piece of wisdom – though I took it for granted for many years without appreciating its profundity.

'No one owns you, I know that.
No one owns me. No one owns anyone.
We just get to borrow each
for a while.'

— Jon Courtenay Grimwood

This understanding of the self can be extended to other areas of our beliefs.

For example, it makes sense to say that 'I have a job' as opposed to 'I am the job'. Yet, when it comes to behaviour, we do exactly the opposite. We behave as if we were the job.

When we fail in our job, we take it that 'I have failed'.

When the job gets outsourced, we feel 'I have no more value'.

By being mindful about your choice of words, you can cultivate a healthy attitude in the core of your being. You are not the role.

With mindfulness, I have learned to look at everything I 'own' – including the roles I inhabit – in a healthy way.

I have learned to understand that nothing is absolutely owned by me. I see myself as a trustee instead. The trustee does not own anything except the responsibility invested in me to play my designated roles well, and take care of the things in my possession.

And while I do not own anything absolutely, I enjoy what I have with mindfulness and wisdom.

ARE WE HUMAN BEINGS OR 'HUMAN DOINGS'?

In the scientific name for our species, *Homo sapiens*, the word *sapiens* means 'wise' in Latin.

This is supposedly our crowning glory.

With our innate capacity to be wise, we created great civilisations. We continually develop new technologies and systems that make our lives better. Our high degree of self-awareness has contributed to our survival, evolution and dominance of the planet.

But are we really so wise? We wage deadly wars against each other, we build societies that oppress the weak, we enact laws that curb our nature, we toil away at jobs that make us sick with stress and anxiety...

At times I wonder if we really deserve to be called *Homo sapiens* after all.

It also seems ironic that although we are known as 'human beings', we are always in a state of 'doing' rather than 'being'.

It appears to me that we are programmed to always do one thing or another.

'WE ARE WORSE THAN ANIMALS,
WE HUNGER FOR THE KILL.'

– LEMMY KILMISTER

Our lives predominantly revolve around either creating or acquiring new things, destroying old or unwanted things, and modifying things to be the way we like.

We also spend quite a bit of time moving from place to place exploring the wonders of new experiences. And after we have rested enough, we look for new things to do.

We have a long 'To do' list. How about a 'To be' list for a change? Try making one like this:

TO ~~DO~~ BE LIST

List of things	How will I try to be?
1. Brushing my teeth	I will experience the sensation of the bristles rubbing against my teeth and gums.
2.	
3.	
4.	

Mindfulness provides us an opportunity to be true to our species' name by introducing the 'beingness' to our human state.

In the practice of mindfulness, the body and mind are in a state where there is neither doing nor non-doing. It provides a great opportunity to 'be' than to 'do', and to discover what we 'are'.

INTRODUCING THE BODY SCAN

Doing a 'body scan' is one of the core mindfulness practices. It is one of the simplest and yet most rewarding of all mindfulness practices, in my opinion.

The body scan is practised by bringing attention to different parts of your body. This practice is valuable for several reasons:

1. Body awareness

Our daily routines have radically disconnected our mind from our body.

We often choose to ignore the sensations of the body as we busy ourselves with our routines. Think of the hurting back, the stiff neck and the tightening chest that we have been ignoring for the longest time.

The body scan allows us to reconnect with our body and its sensations, to 'listen' to our body without judging it.

The body has a life of its own. All you can do is put food in your stomach, and the rest of it is taken care of by your body. You do not have to give an order, 'Digest now'.

The body scan allows us to appreciate this body that has served us so well – without it we would not have been able to come to know and experience the world we live in.

2. From 'doing' to 'being' mode

In doing the body scan, think of your body not as an instrument of *action* but as an instrument for *experience*.

By practising it lying down on the floor, you let go of all the control instincts that you typically exert over the body.

This is a good opportunity to honour your body without exploiting it for any other purpose other than simply letting it 'be'.

3. Attention training

The training you receive while in the body scan is in concentration and awareness, both of which are very useful in life.

Without external objects to focus on, the mind learns to fix its attention on a particular part of our body by being aware of the sensations, as well as to shift that attention to various parts of the body at will.

4. Emotional release

Mental stress has been found to cause physiological symptoms such as tense muscles, aches, insomnia, chest pains, and many more.

One of the ways out of this predicament is to bring awareness to the various parts of the body and in so doing release both the body and mind of its afflictions.

5. Emotional meter

By doing the body scan, you will become sensitive to the relationship between stress, emotional pain and the way it manifests in your body.

When you monitor these sensations as if on a meter, noticing their rise and fall, you may be able to identify issues that are lodged unconsciously in your mind. This is an avenue for great insights into your private universe.

6. Being comfortable in your skin

With your eyes closed and your mind focused, you will not have time to judge yourself.

Over a lifetime, the body goes through three stages: growth, maturity and ageing. Can we learn to accommodate each of these stages gracefully? Can we be comfortable in our own skin?

Yes, we can, by gradually embedding the practice of body scan into our lives.

PRACTICE 2

SHORT BODY SCAN

All you need for this practice (and for all other mindfulness practices) is yourself.

Initially you may want to use an audio track to guide you through the process. (You can download a useful mp3 from www.centreformindfulness.sg)

Then, when it feels right for you, you may like to do this practice independently.

The body scan is practised by bringing attention to different parts of your body in turn.

You start by bringing your attention to your right big toe and then to the other toes. Then you slowly shift your awareness to the sole of your foot, ankles, shin, calf muscles and so on all the way to the top of your head.

Ensure you are in an environment where you have least external distraction.

1. Lie down on an exercise mat or a flat surface comfortably with your eyes closed.

2. Start your practice by mentally noticing the different parts of your body.

3. Prepare a sequence based on the sections of your body, for example:

    - left leg
    - right leg
    - back of the torso
    - front of the torso
    - left arm
    - right arm
    - neck
    - face
    - back of the head

4. Start noticing each of these sections of your body for a minute or 30 seconds before moving on to the next section. (In order not to watch the time during your practice, wait till you've completed the entire body scan before you look at how much

time you took altogether and adjust your pace in your next practice.)

Post-practice questions

- Were you able to notice the different parts of your body?

- Did your mind get distracted?

- Was it easy to do this practice on your own or would it have been easier with a step-by-step audio guide?

DAY 3

WITNESSING

CONSCIOUSNESS

A man was taken to court for embezzling money from his employer.

An eyewitness was called in to report what she saw.

The judge asked if she was involved in the criminal act.

She replied that she had witnessed what happened but she was not involved in it in any way.

Now imagine the complexity of the case if she had been involved.

There is a difference between being involved and being a witness. The witness just reports what happened while those involved actually experienced the event.

In our lives, we can bring the attitude of a witness to all our experiences.

In fact, all that we do in mindfulness practices is to witness and notice all our sensations and experiences.

With a witnessing attitude, pain, pleasure, heat and cold can be reduced to being plain experiences of the sensory organs. You witness them happening without identifying with them. (This is similar to the many roles that you have taken up without identifying yourself with any of them.)

With gradual consistency in mindfulness practices, the intensity of pain, stress and other debilitating experiences can be greatly reduced. This has been shown in many modern research experiments.

'THE CONTACTS OF THE SENSES
WITH THE SENSE OBJECTS GIVE RISE TO
THE FEELINGS OF HEAT AND COLD,
AND PAIN AND PLEASURE. THEY ARE
TRANSITORY AND IMPERMANENT.
THEREFORE, LEARN TO
WITNESS THEM.'

– BHAGAVAD GITA

Furthermore, by adopting a witnessing attitude, one can objectify such experiences without them getting transferred to one's
being and trapping us in emotions and thoughts.

Saying 'I am in pain' is very different from saying 'The body
is in pain'. In the second perspective, you start witnessing the
pain by detaching yourself from it mentally while experiencing
it physically.

Your being beholds these experiences, but it is *not* these
experiences.

I like the analogy of a projector and its projection. The projection on a white screen depicts many images of different colors
and content, but the screen does not change its nature along
with the projected images. All it does is to provide a support or
background for the projected images. Without the screen, the
projection is not possible.

Your mind is like a projection screen, all blank and ready to
receive any sensory experience and to do so without being
altered. It just witnesses these experiences, knowing that they
belong to the body and senses.

As an athlete during my teens, I sustained a knee injury that prevented me from participating in strenuous activities. The injury soon transformed into a larger fear. I would hesitate to take part in any physical sport at all.

While the pain was physical, the fear it created was mental.

A little later in life, as part of my mindfulness practice, I started noticing the pain in my knee. Gradually, the fear of the pain and its possible consequences faded. All that I did was to observe the pain.

Today I jog twice a week and practise postural yoga, setting reasonable limits to my practice. The pain has not completely gone away, but I have learned to live with it. It is no longer a physical or psychological obstacle to my pursuits.

This witnessing ability greatly reduces the impact that any adverse experience has on us. We stop identifying ourselves with our experiences. Instead, we adopt an outlook of acceptance and accommodation.

MINDFUL LIVING

Mindful living is all about bringing the attitude and values of mindfulness into daily life. It enables us to look at life in a different way and discover things that we have missed all our lives.

By leading a mindful life, we live each day as if it is a new one and welcome all its experiences.

Here are eight things you can do to start living mindfully:

'WE ARE NOT INTERESTED
IN THE UNUSUAL, BUT IN THE
USUAL SEEN UNUSUALLY'

– BEAUMONT NEWHALL

1. Practice

The only way to learn to ride a bicycle is to ride a bicycle. No amount of theoretical explanation can make you master riding a bicycle.

It is by trying, making mistakes, and retrying that we master the skill.

Over time, having mastered riding, we are no longer conscious of the riding anymore. We use the bicycle to make journeys to many destinations.

Mindfulness is rather like learning to ride a bicycle. Having mastered it, you can make your journey of life mindful without any conscious effort.

And all of these start with practice. Practice mindfulness daily without fail. Even if it is for a minute, do it.

The brain is like a muscle. The more we flex it, the stronger and healthier it gets. This is due to the neuroplasticity of the brain, which scientists discovered about 50 years ago. The moment we stop flexing it, it withers.

Bring this attitude to all areas of your life, at work, at home, at social events. You can start by:

- mindfully turning these pages as you read

- mindfully listening to people as they speak

- enjoying your cup of tea by mindfully sipping it

It is through these baby steps that we gain mastery without having our focus on the eventual goal of mastery.

2. Being comfortable with silence

I cannot understate the value of silence.

Most of us shun silence because we are not comfortable with it. We often attempt to find something to do whenever we encounter silence.

Try this: Close your eyes now and enjoy the silence for the next three minutes.

Did you enjoy the silence? Or did your mind compel you to do one thing or other to engage your senses? For most of us, it would be the latter.

Somehow we reserve silence for monks and hermits and don't consider it something for us. Yet, we are the ones who need it most, living as we do amid the hustle and bustle of urban life.

Our lack of appreciation for silence could be due to our belief that silence is not valuable economically. It is not going to feed you, earn you money or solve your life problems.

I beg to differ, though. Silence is more valuable for the prime reason that it allows you to feed yourself, earn money and solve problems *more effectively*.

Silence is like the eye of the storm which is absolutely calm in spite of the powerful whirlwind of energy around it.

Silence is like the rest given to a motor or an engine after a long day of ceaseless activity.

We, too, need such rest to calm down, so that we can work with greater energy and effectiveness.

Sleep is definitely an opportunity for rest, but it does not work on our minds as greatly as silence does. Silence is a conscious choice, unlike sleep.

You can make silence available anywhere. All you need to do is shut the door and sit on your bed or your office chair for just five minutes with your eyes closed.

Thoughts will rush in and distract you – do not resist them. Accommodate them like an ocean accommodates all waves.

3. Time with yourself

As a teenager, we enjoy the time we spend with friends and generally people whom we prefer to be with.

But as we grow up, it seems to get harder to exercise this free-dom to spend our time with people that we like to be with.

Instead, we seem to be given fixed roles which come with limited freedom, such as being an employee, a caregiver for elderly parents, a neighbour, a community leader, amongst many other roles.

These roles do not give us much room for choice. We are expected to discharge our obligations regardless of choice.

While it is commendable that we sacrifice our time and energy for others, do we spend enough time with people we choose to be with – and with ourselves? Do we find time to be with friends and with ourselves without an agenda?

Commit to spending time by choice. Go for a walk alone in the park or just sit down with your loved ones or your pets.

4. Relationships

We meet many people in the course of our lives. How do we treat them?

As you interact with people, try your best not to judge them. Treat every meeting and connection with others as an opportunity to accept and accommodate them as they are.

The difference between you and them is just the notion of self-identity, with memories of the past and an agenda for the future.

'FAMILIARITY BREEDS CONTEMPT'

– AESOP

Yes, you are actually not that different after all. In the present, two beings are just 'being'.

The biggest challenge occurs with people who are near and dear to you and those whom you have invested your emotions in. These are the people that we usually take for granted and judge incessantly.

I find that it is easier not to judge my staff than my spouse or parents. That is because these people are so close to us that we constantly judge them for trivial things.

I am sure you are familiar with stories of quarrels over the tooth-brush being placed on the wrong side of the vanity counter or with disagreements over points of view.

We need to cherish relationships by accommodating them without judgment and noticing what is working well in the relationship. Focus more on similarities while respecting differences.

5. Choose your environment

Our environments – whether natural or manmade – have a direct impact on our lives.

For those of us who live in the dense urban jungle, try to find opportunities to walk through parks or look out of your office window to witness the birds on the trees, the unripe fruits hanging on the branches and the squirrels. Observe the plants as you water them and the flowers that have bloomed.

Let your eyes fall on all of nature and let it connect with you.

When I jog in the park near my home, sometimes I jog over to the stream to look at the fishes and turtles. They bring a fresh perspective to life.

Research has shown that people who live amidst nature are happier than those who do not.

So it is good to introduce some greenery into your home, not just for decoration but also for you to observe and spend time with.

As we go about walking from point A to point B or while waiting for the bus or train, we tend to plug into our music or fiddle with our smartphones, sending text messages, browsing social media or playing games.

Take a break from this tendency by choosing to enjoy the journey.

Watch the people on the crowded bus or train. Feel the moving train. Listen to the sounds around you. Notice your thoughts.

Laugh at the judgments that your mind (not you) makes about the guy who looks cool or being jealous over the beautiful lady opposite you.

If you drive, then there is a high chance that your journey is primarily on a fixed route every day.

Maybe you could try a different route once in a while and notice the changes that have taken place. Or perhaps even start noticing with purpose while driving on the same route daily.

6. The present moment

Spend more time enjoying the gift of the present moment. The quickest way to do this is to bring your attention to your breath.

Our minds inevitably react to both thoughts of the past and future. Why not take a break from this routine to be in the present, where there is certitude?

The wonder that you are can only be seen in the present. The universe opens itself in front of you just because you are there to witness it. Witness everything as if it was meant to be witnessed by you.

Bring this attitude in your life by making the first step to notice yourself and your breath.

> 'THE ULTIMATE VALUE OF LIFE
> DEPENDS UPON AWARENESS AND THE
> POWER OF CONTEMPLATION RATHER
> THAN UPON MERE SURVIVAL.'
>
> – ARISTOTLE

7. Listening to your emotions

Instead of rejecting the unpleasant emotions in your mind, witness them like they were never yours.

Like the body, which has a life of its own, the mind too has a life of its own. Like a monkey, our minds can make a circus out of our life experiences.

Just watch those unpleasant thoughts come and go. Emotions have the power to enter your mind, but you hold the power to let them stay or leave.

Emotions are like guests entering your doorway. No guest stays forever. She has to leave someday. If you do not entertain her, she will leave.

Noticing our unpleasant emotions helps us to stay disengaged from those emotions, thus reducing their negative impact.

8. Gratitude

Gratitude is a human trait that we share with domestic animals. We can learn so much from them.

Dogs will not bite the hand that feeds them. They openly show gratitude to us for caring for them.

Similarly, we humans have so much to be grateful for.

I am grateful for the sun, which provides us with light and heat; the air that I breathe; the public transport system that I use every day.

An acquaintance once told me that we should be grateful to the ice-cream man for providing us with the opportunity to enjoy an ice-cream rather than expecting him to be grateful to us for being his customer. What an insightful perspective!

Even if the subway trains break down from time to time, be grateful that you need not travel to work on foot. Or just be grateful that it has served you well for so many years.

Be grateful that you have a team at work or colleagues to inter-act with instead of complaining about their performance.

In all these cases, being grateful is a magic pill that calms down our mental agitation instantaneously.

Gratitude is not just about saying thanks and showing apprecia-tion. It is a way of seeing the world through the lens of our mind.

INTRODUCING BREATHING SPACE

Breathing space is a practice that allows you to check your bodily sensations, thoughts and breathing wherever you are.

A shortened version, known as 'coping breathing space', is especially valuable when your thoughts are starting to move in a negative direction.

It can help you when you are in situations such as:

1. A tense meeting at the office

2. Before an important job interview

3. A heated conversation

4. Before giving a speech

5. Before a competition

6. During a tense business negotiation meeting

7. A stressful situation

8. A sorrowful or shocking event

Just step out of the situation that is making you feel uncomfortable and practise coping breathing space. It will bring your mind back to a mindful state and to the present moment very quickly. All you need is three minutes.

Breathing space need not be practised only when the emotional storm is raging. Instead, it should also be practised when your weather is fine, and the skies are clear, so as to prepare you to cope with the real storm.

PRACTICE 3

COPING BREATHING SPACE

Coping breathing space is best practised in a relatively quiet space.

1. Seat yourself comfortably, either on a chair or a floor cushion.

2. Gently tell yourself that you are now seated with a clear intention to focus on your breathing.

3. Start observing your breathing without trying to change its rhythm or pace in any way.

4. Just notice it with genuine curiosity. There is no goal in this practice except your being in the present noticing your breath.

5. Whenever your mind wanders, bring it back to your breath.

6. Do this practice for about three minutes.

Post-practice questions

- Did you feel calm and collected after the practice?

- How did you keep track of the three minutes?

Whenever you feel stressed, sad, anxious, depressed, or if some other negative emotion is dominating your thoughts, do this practice.

DAY 4

THIS IS NOT A

PRACTICE

I am cautious about using the word 'practice' as it gives the impression that mindfulness practices require you to take deliberate actions against your will or nature. 'Practice' seems to suggest that you need to 'drill' yourself, regularly and purposefully.

This could be a big turn-off for some, the idea that mindfulness as a practice is something to be 'done'.

On the contrary, mindfulness practices are all about 'being'.

Consider how you prepare for bed every night by arranging your pillows, setting the right room temperature and changing into your sleepwear.

All of these only set the stage for your sleep. They do not make you sleep, but rather create the right conditions for sleep to happen. While asleep you are not consciously aware of the pillows, room temperature or your clothes. You just sleep.

So mindfulness practices are about creating the conducive conditions such that mindfulness happens.

This is a key point in mindfulness that many do not appreciate.

Initially, it may appear as if I am setting up an agenda for mindfulness practice, but soon enough you will slip into a mode of spontaneity where it becomes effortless.

To reiterate, practising mindfulness is like preparing for sleep and not the sleep itself.

The practice of mindfulness is also about setting intention, attitude and attention (see Day 1). Do it at a level that feels right for you, without the feeling of being compelled, forced or unhappy.

Hence we say 'practice' for want of a better word. Once we get out of this practice mode orientation, we start enjoying being mindful as being ourselves.

Gradually appreciate that each mindfulness practice is a date with yourself.

MINDFULNESS PRACTICE IS ABOUT
CREATING THE CONDUCIVE CONDITIONS
SUCH THAT MINDFULNESS HAPPENS.

I find more comfort and enjoyment in doing my mindfulness practices alone.

Doing them with another person may pressure the other person to conform to my availability in the day, or vice versa.

Some practitioners of mindfulness have a habit of comparing how they felt during a particular practice. I have also heard of people comparing how long they were in the seat of meditation, and deriving a sense of fulfilment and satisfaction from their accomplishment.

Although this may arguably help in tracking our progress, we end up making mindfulness another item on our long checklist of tasks – with clearly defined key performance indicators!

Do not judge yourself if you have done this, because that's how we have been taught to measure every activity.

All the indicators used at work and in life to measure our 'success' revolve around how much money we have made, how much savings we have accumulated, how much output we have produced, how much time we have shaved off from the time taken to complete a certain activity, and so forth.

We have made this such a habit that we bring the same 'criteria' to our mindfulness practice.

But remember that mindfulness is not something to be 'done', much less a test or a race.

So try to stay away from comparing your practice with others. Instead, you and your fellow practitioners can collectively celebrate the fact that you practised.

And most importantly, practise every day, even if it is just for five minutes.

FOCUSING ON WHAT WORKS

Stephen bought a bouquet of his wife's favourite roses to surprise her.

They arranged to meet at 5 p.m. at the shopping mall, but the bus Stephen was on broke down on the way there.

His wife became anxious at the crowded mall and when Stephen turned up 15 minutes late she spat words of disappointment and accusation at him.

The conversation between them escalated into a battle of words and in the end, the bouquet of roses never changed hands.

One of the great things about the human race is our ability to look at our failures and improve upon them, thereby advancing our civilisation.

In our individual lives, too, we often zoom in on aspects that we feel are in need of improvement, correction, eradication.

'MY ONLY FAULT IS THAT
I DON'T REALISE HOW GREAT
I REALLY AM.'

– MUHAMMAD ALI

However, such an approach to advancement does not tap into our greatest potential. These deficit-focused approaches make us feel miserable about who we are. Any efforts at improvement are then motivated by the need to not feel miserable or insecure.

If you have undergone a performance appraisal at work before, you will know what I mean.

Do you remember the feeling when your boss went through the long list of things that you did not do well and how he kept harping on it? I am sure it was not a great feeling to be hearing about 'What you are not good at'.

Now imagine if your boss spent a larger part of the time with you talking about the things you did well and how that contributed to the success of the department.

How would you have felt? Would you have felt more motivated to improve and excel? Would your mood and emotions be more positive?

This is an asset-based approach as opposed to the earlier deficit-based one. Research at the University of North Carolina at Chapel Hill has shown that people feel more motivated when the conversations around them revolve around what is working for them rather than what is not.

The challenge, however, is that our brains have a natural negative bias that is entrenched in finding fault and focusing on what is not going well.

Like in the story of Stephen and his wife, the delay caused by the bus became the focal point of their conversation. If only they focused on the bouquet of roses instead, the whole situation could have turned out so different.

It takes time and effort to celebrate what is working well in our lives.

In mindfulness we focus on what is right with you rather than what is wrong.

The whole world may judge you based on the many roles that you play in your life, and how you may or may not be up to the mark.

But how about changing that narrative for a second and looking at what you *have* done well?

There are countless things you have done well. There could also be many strengths in you yet to be unearthed in the right circumstances.

'THERE IS MORE RIGHT WITH YOU
THAN WRONG WITH YOU.'

– JON KABAT- ZINN

The difference between seeing the bottle half empty and half full is the attitude of the viewer.

Focusing on what is wrong with us will further preoccupy our minds with what is not fine, and misery follows.

By looking at what works in our lives instead, we can further use that to make our lives better.

Here are some tips on how to flip your perspective:

Deficit-based thinking	Asset-based thinking
I have lost so much money.	From the lesson learnt, how can I utilise my finances and further grow it or explore other alternatives?
I am not effective at leadership.	Can I learn from specific incidents where I have led people to achieve their goals successfully?
I am not a good spouse.	I must have done well or we would not have come this far. I must recollect the great points of our marriage. And possibly keep doing what I am good at.
I am a good-for-nothing.	What are the areas of my life that I felt excited and energised about? Can that help me in uncovering situations which can help me succeed?

Focus on your assets and remind yourself that you are unique. Because you *are* unique. There is no other person like you, and there is a place for everyone in this universe.

LIKES AND DISLIKES

Most of the time, we spend our time doing things that we like, while staying away from things that we dislike.

We do know, of course, that some of our roles require that we do things that we dislike, like clearing the garbage can, or doing the dishes, or even spending time with our family.

There is also this concept that we should go beyond our likes and dislikes. However, that doesn't work, because doing what I like brings happiness and comfort, while doing the opposite brings unhappiness and discomfort.

But yet we know that we do need to do what ought to be done for a variety of reasons.

So what should I prioritise? The sweet drink on the table, which may aggravate my diabetic condition, or the glass of water? I could enjoy that sugary drink, but I might suffer later.

The answer to this is: Do not try to grapple with the rationale behind what needs to be done. Instead, in mindfulness we deal with our issues through the practice of 'non-striving'.

'IN MINDFULNESS, ACCEPTANCE ALWAYS
COMES FIRST, CHANGE COMES AFTER.'

– SHAMASH ALIDINA

So, rather than 'striving' to deal with our issues head-on, which merely creates greater stress and pressure, we approach them indirectly through mindfulness practices.

We all know what is right for us. What we lack is the mental conviction to do what is right. Mindfulness practices strengthen our minds to do just that.

By bringing the awareness of being into our life, we accept ourselves and our supposed issues as they are. As a result, we are better able to make the right choices that contribute to our well-being.

Non-striving is indeed one of the keys to being mindful. Take the struggle out of handling the issues and focus on the practice.

Truly there is no goal as you practise. Just like your breathing, which happens without a conscious goal, you need to anchor yourself to the understanding that you are 'doing for the sake of doing' and not for the sake of a cherished goal.

DEVICE DETOX

I am not sure if you have heard, but humankind has been taken hostage around the world by high-tech intelligent devices. These devices have penetrated into our brains to get us addicted to them.

Yes, I am talking about smartphones, tablets, laptops, smart-watches, and other such devices.

Truth be told, I am not sure if these devices wanted us or if it was the reverse.

This smartphone addiction is a classic case of how an awesome invention robs us of our ability to be with ourselves without any distractions.

I see couples at the dinner table fiddling on their smartphones for minutes without uttering a word to each other.

I see children plugged into their tablets and smartphones for hours (possibly so as to free their parents to do their own thing).

On the bus or train, I see people playing games and watching movies on their mobile devices rather than conversing with others – or just 'being'.

I do not see any problem in these devices as they are not inherently bad. I use a smartphone too.

But how we use these devices can make a significant difference in the way they contribute to our mental and even physical well-being.

Today gadgets have become something that we are connected to by force of habit. Anything that causes the mind to be habitually drawn to it becomes an addiction, and hence it is unhealthy for us.

Being mindful means the exact opposite. In being mindful, we bring conscious awareness into our interactions.

So while these devices are admittedly very useful, we do not need them all the time. This is the difference that we can make in our lifestyle.

Even just witnessing these habitual inclinations can help in drastically reducing our dependence on them.

Then, we should find opportunities to 'detoxify' ourselves of this addiction by putting our devices away at specific times and contexts, for example:

- during meals

- when you are in bed and about to sleep

- when you are walking (for safety reasons too)

- when you are with a loved one

Try also taking frequent short breaks from devices at your workplace. Take a walk to the pantry. Look out of your window at nature or something that is not digital.

INTRODUCING MINDFUL EATING

Mindful eating is a great practice that uses an essential daily activity to bring mindfulness into our lives.

I remember once walking into an eatery looking for my favourite food. Having found it and holding the dish on my tray, I walked over to a table to enjoy it.

The next thing I knew, I had finished all the food and could not remember its taste.

My mind had been wandering all over, thinking about my tasks for the day and my activities for the evening. Even checking my emails on my smartphone (very smart indeed) between mouthfuls.

On other occasions, I have mindlessly eaten so much food while watching a movie. This was a habit for me.

Mindful eating is all about bringing the mind back into eating with full awareness.

I like the way the dishes are served one after the other at Chinese ten-course dinners. It is a great opportunity to bring mindful awareness to enjoying one dish at a time.

Food on the table is a privilege. Let us eat with mindfulness, gratitude and respect.

PRACTICE 4

MINDFUL EATING

You can do this practice with any of your daily meals or even when just having a snack.

First, choose a conducive environment to eat in – one that does not allow you to have a conversation, so that you can bring your full awareness to the meal. Silence is the key, not quietness. You can be silent in a noisy environment.

Place your devices away from sight. Turn off the TV.

When you are about to take your first mouthful, look at the food as if you were looking at it for the first time. Notice the ingredients, the colours, the composition on your plate.

Enjoy the aromas.

Then place the food on your tongue and chew slowly. Really take your time here. Chew for at least 30 seconds before swallowing.

As you chew, pay attention to the flavours of the food. Pay attention to textures as well. Savour the details and nuances of the various components of the dish. Imagine you're trying to extract all the essence from the food.

Engage your hearing too, by listening to the crackle and crunch as you bite into certain foods, and as you chew.

Try this at least once a day, or perhaps with the first three mouthfuls of the meal for a start.

Post-practice questions

- Was this different from how you normally eat your food?

- Did the food taste different when you ate it mindfully? If yes, what made the difference?

- What did you learn from eating the food mindfully?

DAY 5

RESPONSABILITY

There is a part of our brain which dominates our emotional reactions and our actions. It is called the amygdala.

Neuroscientists consider the amygdala to be the least developed part of the brain in terms of its evolution and behaviour. In fact, it is sometimes referred to as the 'reptilian' brain, the oldest part of the human brain.

Why call it reptilian? The reason for such 'negative press' for the amygdala is that it has refused to evolve from the way reptiles behaved, and continues to trigger in us the 'animal' response to fight or flight. These are our instinctual behaviours related to aggression, dominance, reaction and territoriality.

The amygdala dominates most of our behaviour when we are faced with challenging situations. If there is one word that best describes its effect, it has to be 'reactive'. It causes us to be reactive and impulsive.

The Nobel Prize-winning psychologist Daniel Kahneman likens the behaviour of the amygdala to an elephant and our executive abilities to its rider. The reactive tendencies in our brain are very much stronger than our executive abilities. That is how powerful the amygdala is.

We usually do not display these reactive instincts in our daily interactions. But when danger looms, the amygdala kicks in, and we immediately flee, freeze or fight. This happens so quickly and instinctively that we do not notice it.

In the years that I worked with prison inmates, one recurring theme came up: their remorse over their reactive behaviours which landed them in trouble. It was the untamed brain that got the better of them.

None of us are immune from this problem.

However, as human beings, we are endowed with the ability to use the executive abilities of our brain more than the amygdala. This ability resides in the pre-frontal cortex, the part of our brain that controls 'response', as opposed to 'reaction'.

This is what I call 'ResponsAbility', the 'ability' to 'respond' with discretion to the various situations in our lives, instead of reacting to them in a purely 'reptilian' way.

Before you admonish your child the next time for misbehaving, look for the gap between the experience of his/her misbehaviour and your action.

Or perhaps before you take your colleague or staff to task for a job not well done.

Try to look for this elusive gap in every situation. It is elusive because we are so prone to reacting impulsively.

Consistent mindfulness practices help to create this gap naturally. You do not have to look for it anymore. It just happens with every experience.

You will be able to make better decisions in your effort to correct your child or improve your staff's performance, instead of lashing out at them in anger and producing not only no improvement in their behaviour and regret on your part, but also a lasting habit of rash outbursts.

Brain scans have found that regular mindfulness practices change the brain structure: the amygdala shrinks, the prefrontal cortex lights up with activity. This is another great reason for wanting to be mindful.

With consistent mindfulness practice, you will be able to make wise decisions without being carried away by your reactive instincts. ResponsAbility will help you be in control of any situation instead of being controlled by it.

MINDFUL INQUIRY

Mindful inquiry is the process of asking questions so as to see things as they are – clearly, objectively, without judgement.

But while we often inquire about things in the external world, about facts and figures, seldom do we inquire *within*.

When we inquire within, we pose questions to ourselves. These questions allow us to penetrate into the deeper recesses of our minds, and help us understand our own behaviours, emotions and thoughts.

I had a participant in one of my mindfulness workshops, Sophie, who was going through a difficult time. Among other things, she shared that she did not like to be at home in the evenings.

I asked her to do a mindful inquiry on this particular behaviour for the sake of understanding herself better. I encouraged her to write down her observations in her journal.

The next week when she turned up for the class, Sophie was all smiles. She told me that she had found out something about herself.

'THE SCIENTIST IS NOT A PERSON WHO
GIVES THE RIGHT ANSWERS, HE'S ONE
WHO ASKS THE RIGHT QUESTIONS.'

– CLAUDE LEVI-STRAUSS

The first thing she inquired on was why she did not like being at home. Her answer was that she did not find happiness at home. Let us note here that it was an emotion that caused her behaviour.

And what caused that unhappiness? She shared that this feeling had started when her aged mother moved into her home. Since then, she had not had the privacy to spend time with her husband.

She added that her mother was insensitive to her needs, and never gave her the space she needed. These were Sophie's thoughts.

Despite this unhappiness, she looked happy sharing her inquiry with me. As much as I could infer the reason for this, I wanted to hear it from Sophie herself.

She told me that when she asked those questions of herself, she found an awareness about her feelings and her beliefs that she never had before.

In fact, she realised that this issue with her mother was baggage that she had been carrying all her life.

With this new clarity, she saw that she needed to shake these issues off her back. But simply the discovery of the underlying problem was enough to lift Sophie out of her gloom.

She shared this reflection with her husband and felt even better that he understood her better now.

Self-awareness is power. The awareness of your behaviours, emotions and thoughts has the power to induce positive changes in you effortlessly and naturally – without you having to forcefully change yourself. And it all starts with mindful inquiry.

We need to be careful, however, that our inquiry is not for the purpose of finding a victim to blame or for judging ourselves. This is how a court session or a police investigation might be conducted, but not mindful inquiry.

Inquiry is about being genuinely curious. Children naturally display this curiosity when they ask endless questions. As we become adults, we hesitate to ask questions for fear that we appear ignorant.

Asking questions can be truly revelatory for the questioner. For a single question, there can be many answers. Each of them will reveal new perspectives. That's the reason counsellors, psy-chotherapists and coaches ask so many questions instead of telling us what to do.

By asking ourselves questions, we counsel ourselves. Remember Sophie? Be your own trusted friend.

THOUGHTS ARE THOUGHTS

In your mindfulness practices so far (breathing space, body scan and sitting meditation), have you encountered difficulty maintaining your attention? Did your mind wander?

It is natural for thoughts to naturally creep into your head when you start concentrating your mind in mindfulness practices. I remember getting frustrated in my first few practices

In my mindfulness workshops, people often share with me that they are unable to meditate because too many thoughts intrude on them during the practice. I tell them that that is precisely the reason why they should be meditating.

The mind that does not wander does not need meditation. It is the average person like you and me who needs meditation. The nature of the mind is to wander.

Do not expect to stand in the middle of a highway and not see any traffic. The mind is a thought highway. Sometimes you see a truck, sometimes a motorbike or a luxury car. They come in different sizes, shapes and colors. But they are all vehicles, regardless of their differences.

Similarly, treat your thoughts in your mindfulness practices with equanimity.

See thoughts as thoughts. They may enter your mind with different messages, suggestions and even memories of the past. Treat them all the same. They are only thoughts after all – immaterial and passing.

The more importance we give to a thought, the heavier it gets. The heavier it gets, the more it weighs on us, and the more stress and anxiety is induced.

So, welcome all thoughts into your mind during your practices. Do not fight them to leave. Do not force them to stay either. Let them leave when they want.

THOUGHTS ARE NOT YOU

Rose was elated to win the first prize at her university's Innovation Challenge. As she went up on stage to receive the much-coveted prize, her mother Florence, who was sitting in the audience, was overjoyed.

After the presentation, Florence, still beaming with pride, mingled with the other guests. However, she started to attract many disapproving looks as she boasted loudly to everyone about 'her' achievement.

It came to a point when Rose went up to her mother and said, 'Please, Ma, it was I who won the prize, not you.'

We identify ourselves with the successes and failures of our children, spouses, parents and so forth. We feel bad when they feel bad and good when they feel good.

It is a good feeling when some of the gold dust of people we know intimately rubs off on us. It is as if their successes and achievements have become our own. That is probably the reason why people love hanging out with the rich and famous.

This identification happens internally too. We choose to identify with specific thoughts that mean a lot to us.

For some, the thought of being fat will become an identity issue; for others, it could be being poor, or rich, stupid, or intelligent.

It is not that the thought of being fat, ugly or stupid is a problem. It is identifying with that quality that is the problem. When you say 'I am fat', you have made the quality of fatness a defining part of you.

And this limits you to a narrow definition of yourself. It limits your thoughts, your beliefs about your abilities, your relationships with others, and your potential to be a full human being.

You are more than the fatness that you have identified with. You are so much more than that – more than any number of labels can define.

Some of us also identify themselves with the thoughts of others. A single statement made by someone can ruin our day. We feel that our entire self is being repudiated.

In reality, no statement should have the power to ruin our day unless we empower it by identifying with it. So what if someone called you 'incompetent'? That thought remains apart from you until you choose to identify with it.

Thoughts are just thoughts. If we can recognise that, we should also see that thoughts are not us. To identify yourself as your thoughts – or the thoughts of others – is a mistaken identity. Thoughts are what you *have*, not what you *are*.

Mindfulness practices help us to disassociate ourselves from our thoughts. We learn to objectify them and stop seeing them as part of our identity.

Just remind yourself often that 'Thoughts arise in me, but I am not the thoughts'.

LIVING IS A MEDITATION

Since you started reading this book, your life may have become a little more meditative or reflective. I call this 'living in meditation'.

It is not that your lifestyle has now become somewhat like that of a monk. That is not the goal of mindfulness. Nor is living a life of isolation.

Mindfulness is about integrating a meditative approach with your way of life.

I know of people who wake up as early as 4 a.m. in the morning to meditate for 45 minutes before starting the day and retire to bed by 8 p.m.

Then there are people who wake up at 9 a.m. and go to bed at midnight after a meditation sitting. There is no one-size-fits-all method to make meditation part of your life.

Instead of sacrificing your lifestyle at the altar of mindfulness, integrate them both into a harmonious whole, where you do not see living as separate from meditation and meditation as separate from living.

Living in meditation is the spontaneous ability to live life mindfully.

Mindfulness does not require a religious subscription. Although it has its roots in the soils of ancient India among the practition-ers of Buddhism and yoga, it has been a secular practice for more than three decades.

'THE EARTH MEDITATES AS IT WERE.

THE SKY MEDITATES AS IT WERE.

WATER MEDITATES AS IT WERE.

THE MOUNTAINS MEDITATE

AS IT WERE.'

– UPANISHAD

The same happened with yoga, where it has been stripped of its spiritual roots and is now practised widely as a form of calisthenics.

Today the benefits of both mindfulness and yoga are enjoyed by people of all faiths.

It has become a valuable tool in the areas of education, psychotherapy and even staff development.

I have delivered mindfulness programmes to students and teachers, enhancing their performance at school. I have also guided organisational leaders in embedding mindfulness into their leadership style.

More of these contemplative practices are making their way into the mainstream, and I do expect even more to come in the future.

And the best part of mindfulness practices is, the only apparatus you need is your mind. As long as you have one, you are ready to be mindful.

INTRODUCING WALKING MEDITATION

Walking is one of the simplest activities we do. We often do it in a mechanical manner, on autopilot, our minds distracted by thoughts. We hardly observe the way we walk.

In the practice of walking meditation, you become aware of walking again. You start paying attention to the sheer fact of balancing your body – something you'll have taken for granted since you took your first baby steps.

You notice the sensations of the contact between the soles of your feet and the ground. You also notice how the contact brings sensations throughout the other parts of your body.

While the purpose of walking is to take you from point A to point B, in walking meditation you have no agenda except to walk mindfully and experience every step that you take.

In the words of Jon Kabat-Zinn, founder of Mindfulness-Based Stress Reduction, walking meditation is 'walking and knowing that you are walking'.

PRACTICE 5

WALKING MEDITATION

I would suggest that you practise this for the first time in the privacy of your home.

1. Stand up straight, bare-footed, without straining any part of your body.

2. Feel your feet touching the ground.

3. Distribute the weight of your body on both feet evenly.

4. Have your gaze on the floor without straining your neck.

5. Step out with your left foot. Feel it move, feel the heel touching the ground, now the ball of your foot, now the toes.

6. Feel the same as the right foot comes forward.

7. Walk at a steady pace, slightly slower than your usual. When your attention wanders, bring it back to the sensation of your feet touching the ground.

8. Do this for about three minutes.

Post-practice questions

- How was this different from how you normally walk?

- Was it easy to stay balanced while walking mindfully? Were you able to notice the sensations on each foot as you rolled it forward?

- How could you make this an occasional practice in your life?

DAY 6

MEANING

Recent research in the United States has revealed a strong cor-
relation between mindfulness and meaning in life. This lines
up well with other studies that point out that one's happiness is
directly connected to the alignment of one's goals with one's
meaning in life.

The role of mindfulness is to help us be aware of what gives
us meaning.

Meaning in life can be defined as simply finding your authentic self – the self that you truly are. Being authentic and doing
things that align with your authentic self brings happiness. We

may find meaning in raising our children, tending to the family, success in our jobs, or in our spirituality.

I know a lady who finds meaning in serving the needs of her family. To her, feeding her family a good meal means everything. I clearly remember the smile on her face as I saw her go about her chores and the satisfaction in her eyes when someone complimented her cooking.

'IF YOU'VE FOUND MEANING IN YOUR LIFE, YOU DON'T WANT TO GO BACK. YOU WANT TO GO FORWARD. YOU WANT TO SEE MORE, DO MORE. YOU CAN'T WAIT UNTIL YOU'RE SIXTY-FIVE.'

– MORRIE SCHWARTZ

But that does not float my boat. I find meaning in something else. That doesn't mean my meaning is superior or inferior to hers.

We each find our own paths to realise meaning in life. Thinking that someone else's meaning is going to make you happy is not going to work.

It is important that we know what gives us meaning, or we may be on a wild goose chase, forever seeking something or other, not realising that the search itself is the cause of our misery.

At the same time, the discovery of meaning is not something that happens instantaneously. It is the fruit of awareness, particularly awareness of our motives, intentions, strengths, emotions and values. All these give us an idea as to what makes our life meaningful.

And as you will have realised from the earlier chapters (and the chapters to come), mindfulness practices do just that! They enhance our self-awareness.

Through self-awareness, a sense of clarity about yourself will start to appear. You can liken this to being in a long, dark tunnel, seeing a pin dot of light at the end. As you walk slowly towards it, the pin-sized light gets bigger and bigger, and finally you are out of the tunnel basking in the sun.

Finding meaning is just like this. A growing clarity will take place as you keep practising mindfulness.

Importantly, we need to recognise that the rate of progress may vary from person to person.

I remember a few years ago when it suddenly dawned on me that there was a huge disconnect between my strengths/values and my job. It occurred to me that what I really wanted to do was to bring meaning, value and success to people's lives. And that set me on a transition phase for two years before I formally quit my job to become a leadership trainer and mindfulness teacher.

It is interesting that this happened many years into my practice of mindfulness. But for some of my friends this happened early on in their journey.

'THE SEARCH FOR MEANING ROBS
OUR LIFE OF MEANING, SENDING US
BACK INTO OUR DISCURSIVE MINDS
WHILE, RIGHT IN FRONT OF US,
THE LAUNDRY PILES UP.'

– KAREN MAEZEN MILLER

The thing is not to compare how fast you find your meaning compared to others. We need to remember always that comparisons inevitably bring self-judgement.

As much as finding meaning in life is important to us, we should not treat it as an 'urgent' task.

I like this quote from Dwight D. Eisenhower, who was president of the United States in the 1950s: "What is important is seldom urgent and what is urgent is seldom important."

There is a lot of truth is his words. Finding meaning is not an urgent task, in the sense of being an item on your checklist to be done as soon as possible.

That's because the search for meaning can in fact rob us of its meaning. Searching takes you away from being in the present moment.

For the same reason we do not search for some unique experience or sensation in our mindfulness practices.

We learn to live as we meditate. There is no urgent agenda. All we do is to be in the present moment, living it without judgments. And in time we will discover our meaning.

THE WHOLENESS THAT YOU ALREADY ARE

Before I discovered mindfulness practices, one of the problems I experienced was a feeling of inadequacy, incompleteness and fragmentation in my life. A sense that I was not 'whole'.

This sense of something lacking in me made me very uncomfortable and frustrated with myself and my life.

It made me seek out different experiences, in the hope that the sum total of these experiences would make me whole.

But that did not happen.

In fact, it further fragmented my identities, and each of them had their own dreams, goals and desires.

The son in me was competing with the brother in me. The employee within was competing with the volunteer role I played. All these separate identities gave me a sense of inadequacy.

Am I a combination of a hundred identities or is there a wholeness that encompasses these parts?

The answer to this question was discovered gradually as I observed my mindfulness practices. As I kept up with the practices, I started seeing that all the so-called parts or roles were connected through my awareness.

In fact, this wholeness of awareness is what gives all the roles their meaning.

To know that I am whole – not a person with various parts, or a person missing some parts – has been very grounding and meaningful to me.

You are aware of your body, your thoughts, your senses. In the same way, you are aware of things that are outside you – the chair, the temperature, the people, the environment. All of them are in your awareness.

In this mindful awareness, you are just plain being, without any identity. In this being, thoughts, ideas and perception of your body rise and fall.

There are moments in your life when you lose consciousness of your body, such as when you are in deep sleep. In these states, you are just awareness and being, without any conscious ideas or thoughts to perceive.

I find this awareness to be whole because in it I experience all of my experiences.

I am not talking about the conceptions of a soul or spirituality as presented by various faiths. The recognition of awareness is in spite of your beliefs, not at the expense of it.

Seeing yourself as awareness is not an evident fact; it is a choice. Do you see yourself as wholeness and awareness, or do you see yourself as identities? The former allows you to be part of a greater wholeness and helps you deal with life's challenges.

Experiments with mindfulness among people suffering from serious illnesses, for example, have produced interesting results.

As early as the 1980s, terminally and chronically ill patients at the Stress Reduction Clinic at University of Massachusetts

'IN EVERY ATOM, THERE IS
A REFLECTION OF THE WHOLE.'

– JAY WOODMAN

Medical Centre were led through eight weeks of mindfulness training.

At the end of the eight weeks, the patients were able to appreciate their relationships better and were living their lives with renewed meaning. They had found that they could anchor themselves in a wholeness of being beyond their physical ailments. Such is the power of the vision of wholeness.

In the sitting meditation to be practised next, you will learn to be in the wholeness and awareness. You will learn to accept anything in your mental space to 'be' in your awareness.

Therein you will discover the accepting and accommodating nature of your being.

PEACE AND STILLNESS

At the end of the mindfulness sessions that I conduct, I used to ask the participants questions about their practice as they left the room.

After a while, I noticed that the participants would reply very softly, as they did not want to disturb the sense of peace that they had discovered within over the course of the session.

So I learned not to ask questions right after a peaceful meditation session!

I am sure you will feel the same way after trying one or two of the mindfulness practices here.

In the stillness, you discover the inner peace that is always available but encountered too infrequently. You discover more and more of that peace that can be experienced in being with yourself.

With this inner peace, I've found that my mind reacts differently to situations. The rise of anger, hatred and other unwholesome emotions have reduced drastically over the years. My perspectives of situations and events have also changed.

It is not that I am unable to express my feelings. Sometimes you do need the courage to stand up to protect yourself or others in imminent danger. This is very important in the uncertain world we live in today.

This inner peace also allows me to get along better with myself and others. I relate to people very positively. My relationships have improved, becoming stronger and more nourishing.

Confrontational, problem-centred discussions that were frequent before have transformed into energising conversations. Conflicts are resolved swiftly, if not forestalled altogether.

Sometimes I do feel uncomfortable in environments that exude negative energy. But I am able to hold my peace and composure.

In situations where my active involvement is needed, I am able to get excited and energetic spontaneously as a result of my conscious will rather than being a victim of uncontrollable forces.

My friends and family have noticed these changes in me over the years.

Always remember that acceptance comes first, change later. Accept who you are. These changes may happen to you, but do not set an expectation for results. Practise for the sake of practising, and when you do see change, accept that too.

'IF YOU CANNOT FIND PEACE WITHIN YOURSELF, YOU WILL NEVER FIND IT ANYWHERE ELSE.'

– MARVIN GAYE

YOU ALREADY ARE WHERE YOU SHOULD BE

It may occur to you as you keep meditating that in being and awareness, there is no past or future but just the present. All that you have is the present moment.

In recognising this, you will also appreciate that you are exactly where you are meant to be.

And there is no place you can be without yourself in it.

If you do see yourself as awareness, being and peaceful, wherever you go, you will be just that. It is in the present moment that this happens.

I have heard friends say that they are not happy living in this city and want to move to some other place. If you cannot find happiness in one place, I wonder if you can be happy in another.

The reason for change cannot be for want of happiness as that is a problem of the mind and not one of space.

People move for the reasons of functional necessity, financial opportunities, and conducive environment, amongst others.

'THERE'S NOWHERE
YOU CAN BE THAT ISN'T WHERE
YOU'RE MEANT TO BE...'

– JOHN LENNON

These are all perfectly justified and should be done if you feel the need to do so.

But mistaking it for happiness and wholeness is getting it wrong, for you have placed that experience in a future time and place.

All feelings of happiness, joy, fulfilment and contentment take place in the present. And the first step towards it is to recognise that you are already where you should be.

In the present moment, you should discover that you are the wholeness of being.

INTRODUCING
SITTING MEDITATION

Our day begins the moment we get out of bed and start getting things 'done'. The 'human doing' in us does not rest until we go to bed again towards the end of our active day. It sometimes seems we are in a constant race against time.

Sitting meditation allows you to disengage yourself from 'doing' and engage yourself in the 'being' and 'awareness' that you are.

This is a wonderful opportunity to be in touch with the 'being' that has been 'doing' everything all through your life. It is also a respite from your active mind and body.

In the practice of sitting meditation, you will experience moments of peace and stillness. Discovering this will allow you to recognise your being as peaceful, tranquil and still, even amidst activity. This is what I earlier called 'living in meditation'.

Meditation is also one of the rare practices where the idea of gaining something is not there. You are naked and bare, without desire to accomplish anything other than what you already are. It is a wonderful opportunity for self-awareness and non-striving.

PRACTICE 6

SITTING MEDITATION

Sitting meditation is an extension of the breathing space practice introduced on Day 3.

Remember that as we pay attention to our breathing, we are not forcing or manipulating our breathing. Instead, we just let breathing be the way it is and effortlessly bring our awareness to it.

1. Find yourself a comfortable seat.

2. Gently tell yourself that you are now seated, with a clear intention to focus on your breathing for the next five to ten minutes.

3. Start observing your breathing without deliberately changing its rhythm or pace in any way.

4. Just notice it with genuine curiosity. There is no goal in this practice except you being in the present noticing your breath.

5. Do this practice for about five to ten minutes.

If your attention wanders away from your breath, bring kindness to your practice by accepting the fact.

Post-practice questions

• Did you like the practice? Why?

• Was the seat comfortable? Did you have to make adjustments to your seat to be comfortable?

• Were you kind to yourself every time your thoughts wandered?

DAY 7

INVITING ALL

EXPERIENCES

Pleasure and pain – these two experiences dominate our lives. We are driven to seek the one and to avoid the other. We believe that in so doing, we will achieve happiness and be free from suffering.

What we do not realise is that underlying any experience of pain or pleasure is a more fundamental phenomenon:

Experience = Feeling/Thought/Sensation + Judgment

Every experience is a feeling or thought or sensation *interpreted through our judgment*. Pleasure and pain are not inherent in the sensations but a result on our personal judgments superimposed on the sensations.

Whether we deem something a pleasure or pain is primarily based on how conducive we consider it to be to our well-being or to our cherished values and beliefs.

The same sensation could be desired or not, depending on our judgment. The slight pain felt during a body massage is inviting, but a similar chronic pain in your body is not.

We tend to equate pain with unhappiness and pleasure with happiness, which is not always true.

The problem with superimposing judgments is that we may mistake of assuming the pleasurable to be always good and the painful to be always bad. This can result in avoidant behaviour that has the potential to become compulsive.

Think of being mindful as being like an ocean that accepts the waters from all the rivers without rejection. It remains stable in

'A JOY, A DEPRESSION,
A MEANNESS, SOME
MOMENTARY AWARENESS
COMES AS AN UNEXPECTED
VISITOR. WELCOME AND
ENTERTAIN THEM ALL!'

– RUMI

spite of the hundreds and thousands of rivers that ceaselessly flow into it.

Likewise, as a mindful person, we invite all experiences – be they pleasurable or not – as plain experiences. We do so without making any judgments, without assigning value, without labelling them good or bad, desirable or undesirable.

You could be stepping out of your home as the sky slowly turns dark. It is going to be a heavy downpour.

Would that bring frustration and resentment – as the rain will surely spoil your plans for the day?

Being mindful would mean observing the dark clouds with acceptance, and then doing what needs to be done, which is to grab an umbrella before you go.

There is nothing intrinsically bad or good about the rain.

Our judgement about it comes about because of our expectations. We expect that the weather will be always good, that things will always go as planned. By letting go of that, we accept the rain as it is and respond with objectivity.

In so doing, we gain an acceptance of things beyond our control and a greater compassion for ourselves.

With mindful acceptance, every thought or experience is an unexpected visitor. We do not turn them away, nor do we expect them to stay long. Let them come and go.

BEING MINDFUL IS LIKE BEING AN OCEAN THAT ACCEPTS WATERS FROM ALL THE RIVERS WITHOUT REJECTION.

MAINTAINING EQUANIMITY

When something that we did goes wrong, and we feel upset, we are actually bothered not so much by our action itself as by the outcome of that action.

It is the spilled coffee, the failed examinations or the failed relationship that bring negative emotions to our minds.

Similarly, it is the successes, achievements and accomplishments – rather than our actions that produced these outcomes – that bring us positive emotions.

Maintaining equanimity is about keeping the mind open to all types of outcomes, and accepting all outcomes regardless of the judgments we make of them.

Why do this? Firstly let's consider that all our actions may produce four types of outcomes in relation to our expectations.

For example, I might go to a shopping mall wanting to buy a pair of jeans that I've always wanted.

1. The first possible outcome is that the jeans are available for sale at a price that I can afford.

2. The second possible outcome is that the jeans are being sold at half of my budget.

3. The third possible outcome is that the jeans are being sold at twice my budget and hence way beyond what I can afford.

4. The fourth possible outcome is that the jeans are sold out.

Now ask yourself, how might you have responded in each of these four situations?

More often than not, when the outcomes are less than expected, our mind goes into a negative spiral of emotions. We get upset, disappointed, sad or frustrated over such outcomes.

Worse, these emotions often have a spillover effect on other aspects of our lives. They affect those around us, including our loved ones, and can even totally ruin our entire day. All because our expectations were not met.

MAINTAINING EQUANIMITY IS BEING
ABLE TO ACCEPT ANY OUTCOME
WITHOUT MENTAL DISTURBANCE.

But the problem is not with our expectations.

It is impossible to do any action without expecting a result or an outcome. We would not even lift a finger without having an expectation. Desire and expectations are human and hence they should not be seen as a bane.

In fact, the capacity to desire is what drove our civilisations to progress and flourish, to surmount the greatest challenges, and to achieve all our technological advancements.

The real problem is that we are unable to accept outcomes gracefully without mental disturbances.

Maintaining equanimity is being able to accept any of the four outcomes without these mental disturbances, without being swayed by our emotions. It is our emotional reactions that make us act in ways that are less than desirable.

The role of mindfulness is to allow you to accept any of the four outcomes with equanimity.

It is not that you stop being unhappy or happy. Rather, you will not be strangled by these states of mind. You start being mindful of these emotions without the need to suppress your emotions. It is like saying 'My mind is disturbed' instead of 'I am disturbed'.

One exercise that helps us maintain equanimity is to reflect on the insight that every outcome is brought about through the interaction and contribution of multiple variable factors.

Let's say I accidentally dropped a glass of water on the floor, and the glass shattered to pieces. What are the various factors that caused the glass to shatter?

Here is a list of possible factors:

1. The glass had to be hard enough for it to have such an impact on hitting the floor.

2. The law of gravity had to be present or else the glass would not have fallen.

3. The floor had to be a hard surface for the glass to shatter.

4. The height from which the glass dropped.

5. Myself for initiating the event.

Although there were some five factors that contributed to the breaking of the glass, somehow I chose to zoom in on a single factor, myself, as the sole cause of the accident.

This sense of ownership that we have towards all our actions compounds the way we feel towards the four types of outcomes. This happens precisely because we assume that we are the sole cause of a particular effect.

We must bear in mind that this is not an exercise in divesting responsibility for our actions. Rather it is a mental reflection that reduces the load of the sense of misplaced ownership for any given action or its outcomes.

I have no control over the laws of gravity and perhaps little control over that act of negligence when the glass slipped from my hand. Hence the load of ownership is now distributed over many factors including myself.

If you were to extend this thinking to all of your life's activities, you will realise that almost all of them are contributed to and caused by innumerable factors. You are not the absolute cause of every outcome in your life.

As a result of this mindfulness, you will gradually develop both an acceptance towards all your actions and the ability to see things as they are.

As you face different outcomes from day to day, learn to be a witness of your state of mind, and not a prisoner of your judgments.

MEDITATION IS NOT NON-THINKING

There is this widespread notion that meditation is non-thinking. This could be due to the prevalence of modern yoga, which has been touted as a state of no thoughts or a suspended state of mind.

I am quite puzzled as to how a state of non-thinking or a suspended state could bring value to our functional life.

Perhaps it could give you a temporary respite from all your problems, but wouldn't the state of deep sleep be as good as non-thinking then?

I have always been very wary of people teaching that the aim of meditation is to attain a mystical or superconscious state.

This unfortunately reinforces our sense of striving for a change in a future time, as opposed to being in the present.

Such an approach also reinforces our all-too-common state of being 'human doings' rather than human beings.

HAVING A FAR-FETCHED GOAL IN
MEDITATION IS LIKE TREADING A
PATH OF THORNS TO REACH PEACE.
SPENDING YEARS WALKING ON SUCH A
PATH CAN EASILY BE REPLACED WITH
PEACE IN THE PRESENT MOMENT.

Having a far-fetched goal in meditation is no different from any other goal that we set ourselves. Both require you to put great effort into trying to reach that goal.

Such practices have the capacity to create more stress and tension than what they promise to deliver eventually.

It is like treading a path of thorns to reach peace. Spending years walking on such a path can easily be replaced with peace in the present moment.

This is the difference between meditation as conventionally understood and mindful meditation.

In mindful meditation we have no goal or destination. All that we are interested in is being aware in the present moment, noticing our breathing and our movements.

Non-thinking meditation can sound virtuous, especially when it is achieved through much effort. As much as it may be a legitimate goal from the testimonies of people who have derived some value out of it, it is not so in the case of mindful meditation.

Being mindful is not being bereft of thoughts and also not expecting the mind to be full of thoughts. Both of these wear us down.

Being mindful is simply being aware and being anchored in it. I am not searching for anything in my meditation. I am just 'living in meditation'.

I do not aim to suppress any thought or control it, as this would imply the judgment that thoughts are not welcome and unwholesome. In such a meditation you end up measuring and judging yourself as to how successful you are at staying with a mind that is thought-free.

Having such expectations is like expecting the highway to be free of vehicles. The highway is meant for vehicles, and in fact especially for uninterrupted high-speed journeys.

So it is for the mind. The mind is meant for thoughts. It is not meant to be thought-free.

In fact, I have not found anything this easy in my life. Because I am available all the time to myself, I can bring this awareness anywhere and anytime.

As long as I am available, mindfulness is an opportunity.

INTRODUCING
MINDFUL MOVEMENTS

Mindfulness is not all about sitting still but can also be culti-vated while you are in motion.

Mindful movements are different from routine physical activ-ities. In the mindful movements, we bring the attitude of attention and non-judgment into our practice, accepting the body as it is from moment to moment without wanting to change it.

This is a stark contrast to aerobic exercises, hatha yoga sessions or fitness classes, where you are placed in the doing mode.

In mindful movement practices, we engage in gentle stretches and movements. We learn to not challenge and push the body to unnatural extremes. We are not interested in achieving a per-fect posture.

Instead, we do the stretches to our limit and bring awareness into the practice consistently.

While you are at it, you may feel slight discomfort. Instead of judging that sensation, bring awareness to it, and see it as another experience among the many that you have every day. The ability to notice without judgment is what it is all about.

As you continue bringing awareness to your movements, it may become second nature for you to bring this into all your movements throughout the day.

PRACTICE 7

MINDFUL MOVEMENTS

This practice can be done while sitting or standing. The idea is to pay attention to your movements.

1. While seated or standing, gently bring awareness to your body.

2. Do a quick scan of your body from your feet to the top of your head.

3. When ready, raise your left arm slowly and steadily until your fingers are pointed at the ceiling/sky.

4. Gently and slowly lower your arm back to its original position.

5. Do the same for your right arm.

6. Gently lift your left foot off the floor as high as you can.

7. Gently lower your left foot back on to the floor.

8. Do the same for your right foot.

Post-practice questions

- How energised did you feel at the end?

- Do you have a sequence of movements that you can easily remember?

- What sensations did you feel in different parts of your body?

- Did thoughts enter your mind?

DAY 8

COMPASSION AND

KINDNESS

During one of my workshops, a participant told me sincerely, 'If
someone has hurt me, I can't wish them well.'

I responded to her with a smile, to show my acceptance of her
thoughts.

I'm not sure what she picked up from my smile. But one thing is
certain: it's not easy to feel compassion for others all the time.

We are also very critical of ourselves. I remember an acquaintance of mine who committed suicide for being not good enough in the eyes of his girlfriend. I really wished I had spent some time with him the day before.

We could all benefit from a little compassion.

Whether we feel it about others or about ourselves, compassion is one of the most profound feelings that we as human beings have the privilege of.

Compassion is the deep emotional feeling we experience when we witness the sufferings of others. It is about putting ourselves in the shoes of others when they go through pain or difficulty, and imagining how they feel.

Where there is compassion, it is very difficult to judge others or wilfully cause them pain.

In my school days, I was an avid soccer player. During one of our games, a teammate of mine suffered a bad foul and fell to the ground.

I did not get to see the whole episode of him being tackled, and so when I went up to him, I asked, laughing, 'How did you fall?'

In response, he said, 'Instead of helping me, you are having a laugh at my pain?'

This event left an indelible mark on me. I understood that when someone is in pain, the first thing to do is to soothe it a little. This is an act of kindness.

Acts of kindness are the physical demonstration of compassion, an internal feeling.

Sometimes we feel compassion for someone in misery but fail to transform that into an act of kindness. For the person who is suffering, our silence can be deafening.

Kindness is not measured by how much you did, how many dollars you gave, or how many lives you touched. The fact that you did something is good enough.

Your acts of kindness make a difference. Like giving some money to a beggar on the streets, or helping an elderly person with a heavy load or feeding a poor man.

I have never experienced being a failure for being kind. Performing acts of kindness always reminds me of what I am – a human being. I am grateful for being able to feel compassion and wanting to be kind.

I have also been at the receiving end of kindness from people known and unknown to me. This knowledge motivates me to continue being kind, if at all I need reasons for doing so.

'THE WORLD SUFFERS A LOT.
NOT BECAUSE OF THE VIOLENCE
OF BAD PEOPLE. BUT BECAUSE
OF THE SILENCE OF THE
GOOD PEOPLE.'

– NAPOLEON BONAPARTE

How do we cultivate kindness? It's easy if we know how. The trick is to 'fake it to make it' – which was what a wise teacher told me more than a decade ago.

All you have to do is just do it.

By doing it, i.e. practising kindness, you develop the ability to make it part of you. From it being 'faked' at the beginning, it will eventually become genuine and natural to you.

But isn't 'faking it' unnatural? Yes, it is if you are not in touch with your compassionate self. That's the reason why compassion is such a core value in mindfulness. From compassion alone comes kindness.

You just have to keep growing this compassionate feeling inside you, watering it daily with mindfulness practices. You cannot force compassion to grow. All you can do is nurture it and allow nature to take its course. And when your compassion is tended well, kindness flowers.

While it is mostly easy to have compassion for people we love or even for people we are indifferent to, it is harder to have compassion and wish wellness for those who have caused harm to us.

Like the person who shared his feelings with me during the workshop, it is only natural to feel that way.

So in the practice of mindfulness, we bring a meditation called the 'loving kindness meditation'. This practice helps us cultivate and grow the compassionate self in us.

Loving kindness meditation can be used to direct feelings of compassion to people that we often find difficult to have com-passion for.

More importantly, we also need the same compassion to be shown to ourselves. Self-compassion is as important as com-passion for other beings.

In my mindfulness sessions, participants often report that they were not able to keep up with the practice or did not stick to the planned schedule. I remind them to have compassion for themselves and to accept themselves with all their supposed shortcomings – which are nothing but judgments they've placed on themselves.

I also remind them not to forget their intention behind their mindfulness practices. Hold on to the intention dearly and keep the attitude of acceptance as one of the important elements of mindfulness.

I urge you to do the same.

FORGIVENESS

Forgiveness is another difficult thing for us human beings.

In the past I found it very hard to forgive people who had wilfully done me harm.

But then I asked myself if I had done the same to others, either consciously or unconsciously, and the answer was definitely 'Yes'.

I wished that those people who had been hurt by my actions and behaviour could forgive me.

And if I was deserving of forgiveness, surely those who had harmed me deserved to be forgiven too. I am no different from them.

As I keep reflecting, I realise that forgiveness doesn't mean we are validating the wrongful actions that people have done to us.

All we are doing is letting go of the unwholesome feelings that we have harboured since – the bitterness and hurt that arise anew each time we recall the wrongs. It doesn't make sense to let these negative feelings continue to affect our well-being long after the incident has passed.

We need to let go of the pain by forgiving those who have hurt us.

And the time to do that is right now.

Take a pause from reading this book and spend the next minute forgiving someone whom you have always wanted to forgive. How does it feel?

In experiments at the University of North Carolina at Chapel Hill, it was found that practising loving kindness meditation

'We must develop and maintain the capacity to forgive. He who is devoid of the power to forgive is devoid of the power to love. There is some good in the worst of us and some evil in the best of us. When we discover this, we are less prone to hate our enemies.'

- Martin Luther King

increased positive emotions and decreased negative emotions. I urge you try out the practice at the end of this chapter.

I AM ALWAYS A WORK-IN-PROGRESS

I take comfort in telling anyone I meet that I am a work-in-progress. I am not a statue that was carved and sculpted to be a perfect masterpiece. I am still being moulded, and forever it shall be so.

I am ready to be remodelled in the hands of the world's greatest sculptor, time.

In the present moment, I let myself be crafted by my intention, attention and attitude.

I am not perfect, as a perfect being is but a figment of the imagination. Perfection is always a judgment in terms of thoughts, feelings and behaviour. In my state of being, there are no judgments.

All that I am is meant to be in the present moment. And so are you.

Seeing yourself as a work-in-progress allows you to make mistakes and learn, to fail and keep trying, and finally to accept that you are not some statistic on the wall of perfection.

You learn to accept yourself as a being capable of feeling pain but not be susceptible to it. You learn how to fail but not be a failure. To be successful but not be elated. To be happy but not always. To find purpose in things that may change and perhaps accept purposelessness too.

The only thing you are certain of is that you are awareness and that you are aware of all that is happening to your body-sense-mind complex.

I am a work-in-progress. There is no performance appraisal, there are no KPIs, there are no goals. All I know is that I practise mindfulness with sincere intention.

HOW ELSE CAN MINDFULNESS HELP YOU?

Research over the last few decades has shown that mindfulness practices benefit you in many ways. They can:

1. **Improve your mental health**

    As your brain learns to *respond* rather than *react* to situations, you will find your stress levels reduced, emotions regulated and resilience strengthened. Your emotions and thoughts become healthier, with less dependence on external stimuli for support

2. **Increase your happiness**

    Research around the world has found that people who meditate are in general happier than people who do not. Mindfulness reminds us that happiness is now, not in the future.

3. **Improve relationships**

    Relationships thrive in a space of non-judgment, respect and acceptance. When two people come together with mindfulness, the relationship grows in value, bringing positive emotions and genuine love.

4.   **Increase positive states of mind**

When something goes wrong, our minds tend to obsess over what caused it and who to blame. With mindfulness practices, we can recover from this inherent negative bias in our brain and look at situations more positively.

5.   **Boost creativity**

Creativity lies in the executive regions of the brain. And mindfulness works precisely in that region. Now you know the reason why Google launched mindfulness programmes for its staff!

6.   **Improve your attentional and working memory capabilities**

With the focus on paying attention being a major part of mindfulness practices, you will be able to concentrate on tasks more effectively. The ability to retain what you have learned is also enhanced.

7. Regulate your eating habits

In eating mindfully, you become more deliberate and prudent about the choices you make in your diet. Mindfulness also slows down your eating function, allowing the stomach to communicate to the brain that it is full, so that you do not end up over-eating.

8. Reduce depression

Mindfulness has been used as complementary therapy alongside medication to help people overcome depression. This happens with acknowledging the mood disorders that are associated with depression. By learning to develop a mindful relationship with them, depression is reduced as a result.

9. Reduce addictive behaviours

Addictive behaviours (e.g. smoking, alcohol, drugs) have been seen to decrease with mindfulness practices. The mind is able to achieve reduced dependence on these substances and greater resilience to see one through the withdrawal symptoms.

10. **Reduce chronic pain**

   Mindfulness saw its earliest successes in people dealing with chronic pain. With eight weeks of mindfulness training, patients were found to have increased ability to respond to pain rather than reacting to it.

11. **Enhance resilience**

   Psychological resilience is the ability to adapt and cope in adverse conditions. People in high-stress occupations have found themselves more resilient with mindfulness practices.

12. **Reduce stress**

   Research has shown that mindfulness can reduce and prevent stress. This is one of the most immediate and readily recognisable bene-fits you'll notice from your practices.

13. **Reduce anxiety**

   Anxiety is a phenomenon that is rooted in future outcomes. With mindfulness, the mind learns to be in the present, thus reducing the ill effects of anxiety.

As you get motivated by the benefits of mindfulness practices, it is important that you remember that these goals are destinations. While they are good reasons for starting on mindfulness practices, they should not be the pivot of your practice.

It is always the present moment that you should be focusing on as you take the journey to your destination.

PRACTICE 8

LOVING KINDNESS
MEDITATION

As you read the following lines out loud, bring the emotions and feelings that express the same intentions. Pause after saying each line and notice those emotions within you.

May I be well

May I be happy

May I be healthy

May I be free from suffering

May you be well

May you be happy

May you be healthy

May you be free from suffering

May all be well

May all be happy

May all be healthy

May all be free from suffering

May all be well

May all attain peace

May all achieve completeness

May all be happy

May all be happy

May all be healthy

May all see goodness

May none suffer

May all overcome their obstacles

May all see goodness

May all attain their cherished desires

May all be happy always

May I be able to pardon all living beings

May they always be able to pardon me

May there be friendship amongst all living beings

May I have no hatred of anyone

WHAT NEXT?

I would like to thank you for completing this eight-day journey with me.

I sincerely hope that this experiment with mindfulness has been insightful and rewarding for you. If you discovered just one new thing about yourself during these eight days, you have taken a great step forward.

If you found this book valuable, please do share it with others. Mindfulness gets dusty the moment you shelve the practice – so it is with the book.

If you would like to continue your mindfulness journey, please consider attending a longer course or workshop on mindfulness.

These courses, spanning up to eight weeks, are held all around the world. You will spend two hours of your time per week with a mindfulness teacher. The courses will help you greatly in embedding the mindfulness attitude in your life.

You can find more about the workshops by doing an internet search for mindfulness programmes in your locality or visit my website (www.centreformindfulness.sg).

Do meet the teacher and have a chat about how you would like the workshops to help you. Make sure that you are comfortable with the teacher before embarking on your journey.

Thank you for picking up this book, and for your courage in trying out these experiments.

Most of all, may you be well, may you be happy, may you be healthy, may you be free from suffering. This is all I wish for you.

BIBLIOGRAPHY

Alidina, Shamash. *The Mindful Way Through Stress.* London: Guilford Press, 2015.

Boyce, Barry (ed). *The Mindfulness Revolution.* Boston: Shambhala, 2011.

Csikszentmihalyi, Mihaly. *Flow: The Psychology of Optimal Experience.* New York: HarperCollins, 1990.

Kabat-Zinn, Jon. *Full Catastrophe Living.* New York: Bantam Books, 2013.

Kahneman, Daniel. *Thinking, Fast and Slow.* London: Penguin Books, 2012.

Lyubomirsky, Sonja. *The How of Happiness.* New York: Penguin Books, 2008.

Seligman, Martin. *Flourish.* New York: Free Press, 2011.

Siegel, Ronald, D. *The Mindfulness Solution.* London: Guilford Press, 2010.

Solms, Mark and Oliver Turnbull. *The Brain and the Inner World.* New York: Other Press, 2002.

Sternberg, Esther, M. *The Balance Within: The Science Connecting Health and Emotions.* New York: W.H. Freeman and Company, 2001.

ABOUT THE
AUTHOR

Kathirasan K is an established mindfulness teacher with a background in organisational development, leadership and education. He has over a decade of experience in teaching contemplative practices, and training teachers in meditation and philosophy.

A certified yoga instructor, he is currently doing doctoral research in the subjects of yoga philosophy and meditation.

Kathir is Director of the Centre for Mindfulness, which conducts courses, talks and workshops on mindfulness, and delivers tailored training programmes to MNCs, government agencies and educational institutions.